Live This Feeling

Live This Feeling

Michelle Bonfils

poems

Copyright © 2021 by Michelle Bonfils.

All rights reserved. No part of this publication may be reproduced, distributed, or transmitted in any form or by any means, including photocopying, recording, or other electronic or mechanical methods, without the prior written permission of the publisher, except in the case of brief quotations embodied in critical reviews and certain other noncommercial uses permitted by copyright law.

Live This Feeling / Michelle Bonfils

Published by Pictures In Ink Press, Los Angeles, CA

Paperback ISBN: 978-1-7377295-0-1
eBook ISBN: 978-1-7377295-1-8

Designed by Olivia M. Hammerman
ochbookdesign.com

*To all the people who broke my heart—
If I imagined my life without you,
these poems wouldn't exist.*

Contents

Nervousness
1

Crowded Bar
3

Safe
5

Angel
7

Under Running Water
9

Black
11

I'm Only Sleeping
13

Spaceland
15

Sleep In
17

Yellow
19

Sidewalk
21

Half-Drawn
23

Hi-Fi
25

If You Decide To Leave Your Wife
27

Two Cigarettes
31

Love Like That
33

World Of Pretend
35

So Good That We Know
37

Brilliant Red
39

Closed-Mouth, Tight-Lipped
41

I Give You
43

Live This Feeling
45

You Just Sit There
47

Moses
49

Pride, The Finale
51

Weather
53

Buttons
55

Unopened Letter
57

Swim In Defeat
61

Sahara
65

Settings
69

Playlist
73

Acknowledgements
75

About The Author
77

A Note On The Type
79

Live This Feeling

Nervousness

This nervousness
brings upon the urge
to vomit the words
stuck in this head.

This nervousness.
This cave set deep
at the end of this winding road
I can't drive straight on.

But I get there.
I reach it and it's bliss.

Meet me there.

I promise you won't lose your way.
For I've laid a trail of petals,
of thoughts that tease you to come closer.
Brighten the light that after time shines so dim.

This nervousness.
This ivy grows thick.
It hangs beautifully over my mouth
like a warm blanket.

Drive to me.
Cut away these leaves,
these petals,
these thoughts of promise.

Set this nervousness free.

Crowded Bar

The time in that crowded bar when you
turned me around and held me close,
held me tight because you liked that song.
That song that played for only us.
Hovered around only us in that crowded bar.

The time the people in that crowded bar all
stopped to look at the perfectly mismatched
couple under the colored spotlights that
colored our eyes through stale cigarette smoke.

We sat at the crowded bar, where I picked up
your self-wounding words as they fell from
your wet, whiskeyed lips and held them
out of your reach. If only for one night.

If only for tonight.

You asked me why I was the way I am, and
why I said the nice things I said, but
I could not speak my answers loud enough
for your drunken ears to hear me.

Not in that crowded bar.

All I could do was look at you with sober eyes,
wrap around you my loving arms, and
carry you out of that crowded bar.

safe

That night you buried your face in the nape of my neck
held my hands so tight I thought they would break
wrapped yourself around me so I wouldn't escape

You said—
I make you feel safe.

Angel

I am your angel.
I am your knight in shining armor.
Though I wear it over a dress,
I can still curtsy like the rest.

I will lead you in the steps to this dance
you are made to dance.
To the song that never seems to end.

Take hold of my hand.
I won't let go.
I can't comprehend that command.

So when your head becomes
too heavy for you to hold,
I will place my hand under your chin.
I will keep you straight.

And when you are old,
and I start to go gray,
I will rock you to the steady rhythm
of the sunset.

Under Running Water

I held my breath when he held my hand.
He took my breath when he kissed me.
Then he left the room to wash his hands.

He returned with a medley—
words he constructed under running water.
I looked away not to listen.

To our perfection—
>*We have a real connection.*
To what we shouldn't do—
>*I'm too old for you.*

He walked closer to me out of sorry;
out of pity for the kitty
that got caught in his trap.

As his hand reached out to turn my face
to face his face,
he looked at me with sympathetic eyes.
The look that left me empty.

Yet, he stood proud—
my breath dangling out of his corduroy jeans back pocket,
my smile under his right foot,
and my heart still lays at his doorstep.

Black

Friends call.
Their voices sound like white noise machines.
I haven't washed my hair for days.
Pearl Jam's *Black* plays in the background on repeat, and
the last words you said to me
are splitting apart my brain.

I haven't eaten.
I've barely spoken.
The TV's on, but I can't see nothin' through all this cryin'
and gaspin' for air.
My arms reach out for you,
but you're not there.

Oh God, it's gonna be like this forever, isn't it?

I'm Only Sleeping

Listening to *Revolver*, I turn myself over.
I'm Only Sleeping, you start singing in my ear.
My eyes too heavy to open and realize
your heart was too heavy to hold.

I'm only sleeping.
       Don't wake me up.
I'm only dreaming.
       Don't wake me up.

The first time I saw you
I knew—
the last time I'd see you
wasn't far away.

When that time came
there was nothing I could do,
but say all the right words
in all the wrong ways.

I wanted you to love me
the way I loved you.
Was that too much to ask?
Were my actions too difficult to grasp?

Holding hands and first kisses
at 2 o'clock in the morning
on empty streets;
under their lamps.

Do you remember any of it, still?

I'm only sleeping.
      So, don't wake me up.
I'm only dreaming.
      I don't want to wake up.

Spaceland

Standing here, waiting patiently
in a dark room filled with smoke,
and strangers.
Watching a band that's unknown that
I don't remember paying to see.

Everyone stands around me like
they're someone waiting to be seen.
But they're no one.
They're not in my head.

If I could count the people in my head,
maybe I could pick one and be one.
Someone real.
Someone new.

Instead, I'm someone else.
Someone different.
Someone strange.
Someone drunk.

Who needs another drink?

There's a boy at the bar
standing there, waiting patiently
in a dark room, filled with smoke,
for someone
just
like
me.

Sleep In

Sometimes you just wanna sleep in.
Especially after nights when
you stay up late drinking.

Dogs bark to be let out.
You throw the covers over your head to
keep the sun out.

Sometimes you just wanna sleep in.
Get back to dreaming
and avoid all this feeling.

Yellow

SALVATION IS YELLOW

Glowing above a sea of noise.
Growing deaf in the shadows of the bar.

SALVATION IS YELLOW

Lights flickering above.
Waiting for something to happen.
Anything to happen.
Anything to lift me high.

SALVATION IS YELLOW

Floating above the sea of noise.
Deafening tones are blinding.

SALVATION IS YELLOW

Sidewalk

Down in the basement of some bar.
A friend on my right passes me her guitar.
A boy on my left turns to me and smiles.
A cue for me to stay and play for a while.

He said, "Do you know any Hank Williams?"
I said, "Oh boy, do I ever!"
"Okay, follow my lead and we'll play it together."

His fingers when from strummin'
to holdin' my hand in his
to talking sweet nothin's in my ear.

No words I remember in particular.
Just what I needed to hear.

Half-Drawn

He crept in like the sun
under a half-drawn window shade.
The one I can't get up to pull down all the way.

He crept in that afternoon.
Disturbing my day's dream.

He crept in unafraid.
Straight back and proud.
Waking me.
Violating every scene
my imagination played out.

He crept in.
Making it dark.
Making me sad.
Making me cry.

Making me want him again.

Hi-Fi

Running around the East Village.
Drunk and not a care in the world!

Every night, the smell of whiskey.
God, it was all so easy!

Nights when names had no meaning.
Rings on fingers meant less!

We fell into each other's bodies.
Fell asleep in each other's stories.

We woke up saying,
This can never happen again!

Then again, *in a night or two—*

We find each other running around
the East Village.

And do it all over again!

If You Decide To Leave Your Wife

I spend hours talking myself out of you.
Then I see you again, and it starts all over again, and all
that talkin' I was doin',
meant a whole lot of nothin'.

Here we are.
You and me at the same bar.
This time, your wife is here.
So pretty. So petite.
Nothing like me.

She sits closer to me than you do—
Throwing pretty eye daggers over her shoulder as you mind your manners.

I know she knows.
She knows I know she knows.

You see, even though she came with you,
she's here tonight for me.

She's come to protect her home from the big bad wolf
who, with a big deep breath and a great big smile, can
blow it all down.

But in my defense, she doesn't know that I spend hours
talking myself out of you.
I may as well be an evangelical preacher shouting out
messages from God on a street corner, because—

All this talk goes unheard.
All these words—
they're all just words making me weak.
Maybe it's the heat.

I stumble around this place in a daze.
I pray that you and I will be real one day.
But if that happens, people will get hurt.
They'll be mad as hell and blame me for everything.

But sometimes you have to hurt the ones around you
for true love to be free.

It's worth it in the end.
I know that.
You know that.
She knows that, doesn't she?

Let's just say you decided to leave your wife.
Would you find me a suitable replacement?

Okay, hold on—I'm getting carried away.
Where was I?

That's right.

Here we are again.
You and me at the same bar again.
Your wife's gone home to take care of your family and
you are standing across the room from me.
People are all around us and in between.
You bob and weave, trying to get my attention
as I write little poems down on beer-stained napkins.

Do you have any idea what's flowing out of my pen?
What's spilling out of my heart?
Are you standing there, watching me, realizing I may be the girl who can turn your whole world around
and tear your life apart?

But if you counted all the hours that I talk myself out of you, you'd be counting for days.
There's no point really.
All the math will make you weary and leave your eyes blurry, because—

Every time I see you, it starts all over again.
Every time I see you, I fall back in love again.
And all that talkin' I was doin'
meant a whole lot of nothin'.

I know that.
You know that.
She knows that.
Doesn't she?

Two Cigarettes

I smoked two cigarettes in an effort to kill my appetite for you.

It only made me thirsty for your tongue.

Love Like That

That night you told me how much you loved my body, I tensed up with your every touch.

Wishing I knew how to love like that.

World Of Pretend

Sitting in silence while you speak your stories.
I wonder how you keep going back to him;
for the abuse and the rage and the fuck you give when
you don't touch.

Don't you see you are failing?
Withstanding the infrequent touch of his hand, you
find it promising keeping yourself untouched for nine
months.

While your cheeks shine tear-stricken
under eyes of blue. In this world of make believe, you've
learned to keep your songs so true.

You're gonna live to be one hundred, you know.
If you don't lose yourself first in his power.
Keep that phone close to you,
'cause he can call at any hour.
Answer promptly or
he'll take it all away from you.
And that is your biggest worry.

But remember—
He sleeps in another woman's bed.
He falls asleep at the bar.
When you're not there to soak in his fury,
do you think he cares where you are?

You long so badly to be touched.
To be fed words of love that never end.
In this world, you want only his touch.
His touch in this world of pretend.

So Good That We Know

I stood across from you.
Ready for you—*the way I was ready for them.*
Wanting from you—*what I wanted from them.*
Knowing that it wouldn't be right,
but it was Opening Night!
And this was the first of many.

We stood on the stage.
Bright lights shining down on *us*.
The you and the me that wasn't really *us*.
Styled images that mirror *us*.
An audience that approved our performance.
Reviews that said *we* were good together.
Too bad *we* aren't together.

So good that we know.

You stood up and said your lines.
Said them loud so everyone could see.
I stood down and awaited my cue professionally.
Knowing that both of our names would never fit on the light up marquee.

It wouldn't be fair—*it wouldn't be right*.
Just like that night when w*e* laid there.
Naked bodies in your bed.
I was coming to the thought of *us*
making it in New York City!
You came, rolled off me, stood up
and got dressed.

But it's okay with me.
It's okay that it didn't turn out the way—*I hoped*.
It was rushed. It was forced. It was true—
for only a moment on that stage.
Then that moment escaped.

We took our bow and the curtain closed.

Brilliant Red

I wear this brilliant red on my lips
to cover their quiver.

I wear this brilliant red on my lips
as a disguise to distract you from the blue in my eyes.

I wear this brilliant red on my lips
as a dam to stop the river that flows out of me when
I'm not careful.

Closed-Mouth, Tight-Lipped

How many secrets do you keep in your mind?
How many truths do you hold in your heart?
How heavy are your shoulders from carrying the burdens of others?
Can you count the times you've planted your face in your pillow to scream—
This week?

You can walk around closed-mouth, tight-lipped for days before they ask—
How do you feel?

You turn and answer them with a smile.

I Give You

I give you my words—
>I never chose them wisely.

I give you my promises—
>I broke them repeatedly.

I give you the tears—
>I cried over you nightly.

I give you the poems—
>I wrote about you incessantly.

I give you my thoughts—
>May they make you happy.

I give you my dreams—
>May they come true for you without me.

I give you my heart—
>For all it's ever done is love,
>>unsuccessfully.

Live This Feeling

I'm lying next to him in the dark.
My thoughts are the only sound besides his breathing
and the cars driving on the street below.

I'm lying next to him naked.
My body is shaking under the sheets.
I want so badly for it to be tomorrow.

I'm lying with a rock the size of his fist
pushing down on my chest, and I'm trying my best not
to think of the past. All the times before this that
foretold this time wouldn't last.

I'm lying here fighting off my mind's listing of
all the things that are wrong with me.
Wishing for him to turn around and touch me.
I wish he would just turn around and hold me.

I'm lying here thinking, I did this all for nothing. Flew
across the country for a man who would rather embrace
a bag full of feathers right now than my body.

I'm lying wide awake next to his sleeping.
The heart in me is so fast in its beating.
My eyelids are so heavy they want to fall.
Tomorrow when he wakes up, whatever time this was
won't mean anything at all.

I should leave.
I know I should get up and leave.
But I want to live this feeling.

You Just Sit There

Words don't write.
Voices can't speak.
My silence stumbles over the table onto you wearing
that loud red shirt; one would think you'd have
something interesting to say.

But you don't.

You just sit there as my questions form unasked.
My fear remains unmasked by you who has no need for
words, for words mean more unsaid.
Still, I can't shut you up or out of my head.

As you watch me crumbling,
you just sit there.

Moses

Black eyeliner.
Red lipstick.
Chain smoking cigarettes.
Driving down Sunset,
high on champagne and Vicodin,
to the bar with the butterflies
stuck to the ceiling.

I enjoyed it all—
Self-destructing.
Laughing.
Taking turns reading poetry
out on your balcony.
Having a ball.
What I would give to do it all over again.

But only with you, my friend.

Pride, The Finale

I walk into the bar.
The bar I've been to so many times before.
This time it's different.
No one is with me.
Pink Floyd singing, *Hello?* serenades my entrance.
No one notices as I try to order a drink.
I have money. I'll pay this time.

I used to command this place.
People would come just to talk to me.
Buy me a drink. Take me home.
Now, no one offers me a seat.

There's an empty table and it's in the corner by the popcorn machine.
It has one chair and it's facing the wall.
Popcorn has spilled all over the floor and is sticking to the bottom of my new shoes.

There's a mirror in front of me and I can't stop looking at my reflection.

Is this person really me?

I cut off all my hair earlier because I was sad.
Maybe if I look different, I'll feel different.
Then things could be different.
But it's not working.

Maybe I shouldn't have pushed you so hard.
Maybe I should've listened.
Maybe we should've done what you wanted to.
Maybe I should have asked.

All the maybes are sitting here with me,
reminding me that it's too late to take it back.
It's too late to change it.

Weather

I talk in my sleep.
I call out your name.
The sheets fell off the bed again.
I have only myself to blame.

Mornings aren't warm enough
for this cold body alone.
No sleeping face to look at.
Not since you've been gone.

As the seconds tic away,
I watch the big hand overshadow the small.
I know I have the strength to leave this place.
I just can't find the strength in me at all.

Because I miss you more than ever.
Your sweet kiss on my wrist.
My hat flies off in this weather.

Please come back!
Spend one more night with me!

I insist!

The Times pile up on my doorstep.
The news just passes me by.
I could look out the window for a story.
Instead, I just sit here alone in the dark and I cry.

Because I don't feel like getting up anymore.
Not unless you show up knocking at my door.
Because I don't want to love anyone else.
I refuse to love anymore.

I miss you now more than ever.
More than I did yesterday.
I don't know if I'll ever get over you,
or why you left me this way.

Buttons

Looking the way you do,
you don't act the way you should.
Words sing from your mouth, but
you'd speak too, if you could.

You told me stories of how they
picked you up and held you high.
How your mold's been made
now you don't even try.
Yet you still do.

I was the one you let in.
Now you tell me I can't stay.
You say I push your buttons?
Sorry, I thought they said play.
Guess they weren't the right ones.
Fine.
I'll shut up.
I'll go away.

But don't you look at me with those blue eyes.
Don't you touch me with that soft skin.

Don't you sing those sweet words that keep reeling me back in.

Because I heard all your songs before.
Last year when you were on tour.
And I made my decision—
I'm not going to listen to them anymore.

Unopened Letter

Flirting with the past—
The parts that screwed you up and
the face that didn't last—
Because right now you'll do anything
to feel anything at all.
And he was the last one to make you fall.

There's a letter from him laying on the table, unopened,
and you're staring at it with hope-filled fear that it
might have wishes to reconnect. Even though you know
you shouldn't.

Go ahead.
Tear it up into little, tiny pieces like he tore your heart
up into a million pieces.
Go ahead—Throw it in the trash.

Forget about the time you danced with him
inebriated and in love.
Forget about the night you sank into each other on the
dance floor, then tried quietly to slip out the back door,
as everyone pleaded with you to stay and have fun.

Oh, but remember the night when he held your hand
so tight and kissed you so hard that he bit your lip.
Oh, remember the night he went outside for a cigarette
and kissed your best friend.

It's been three years since then, and now you're sitting
at the table in your kitchen with this goddamn letter in
front of you—
And it's from him.

Whatever he's written means nothing.
Because it took you way too long to get over him—
Countless bottles of whiskey.
Cartons of cigarettes and dancing alone in bars all over this
goddamn city.

Still, you wonder-
What if it says he's sorry?
For making you flirt with the past.
The parts that screwed you up.
The face that didn't last.

Because right now you'll do anything.
To feel anything.
At all.

Swim In Defeat

If you knew what to do—
What you should have done to begin with.
Would you do it?

If it meant you could stay asleep though the night—
No noises to wake you.
No voices from the past.
No faces of the dead.
Would you do it?

If you knew the answer to make it all go away—
would you say the words aloud?
But in a different order this time because
the last time left you sleepless, your face wet.

Words can move mountains.
Words can part seas.
If you use them right—
They can make you happy.

But when you're nervous and all you can think about is
the outcome—

The one that you played out so perfectly in your head.
Now everyone's in place.
It's the right time.
Is it the right time?
It's never the right time.

The stars shift.
The moon follows.
The spotlight moves upstage to down
leaving you in the shadows.

You speak your lines.
You yell your lines!
But your tongue and your lips and the red that paints
them get in the way.
They all look at you in silence.
Your voice cracks to follow.

Then it's quiet.

Your eyes shift—

In focus/Out of focus.
In focus/Out of focus.
To sleep.

You awake in a dream.
You're in your house on the hill—
the one by the sea.
So far up in the sky that the
sound of the waves
mist from the waves
smell of the waves
can't reach you.

All you see are those eyes.
The ones from the street.
The ones that saw you first.
The ones that waited for you—
To be aligned with you.
Those eyes that closed
and opened and closed
on the third blink.

Those eyes of the past that reincarnate
year after year after year.
Those pale blue eyes.

You were dead when you saw me.
Yet, you still let me swim in your sea.

Sahara

Buried all my broken hearts
right here under my feet.

Deep down under the sand
that lifetimes ago was a sea.

Flew halfway around the world on a feeling
that was entirely arbitrary.

Drove miles for days
just to ride hours into the desert
on the back of a dromedary.

As the sun began to set,
I climbed the tallest dune.
I caught my breath, and
watched the rise of the moon.

The colors that changed in the sky
were extraordinary.
The tears that fell from my eyes
were necessary.

My heart beat loudly.
I was exactly where I needed to be.

In the middle of nowhere
on this great big earth.
Contemplating all that my life was worth.
Feeling absolutely free—

    Finally.

Live This Feeling

Settings

The following locations serve as settings to some of the poems contained in this collection. Poems that are not listed below did not have a location in mind when written.

Crowded Bar: Goldfingers Bar, Hollywood

Safe: The Black Cat, Silverlake

Under Running Water: His first apartment on Griffith Park Blvd

Black: My apartment in Los Feliz

I'm Only Sleeping: My bedroom on Harold Way

Spaceland: Silverlake

Yellow: Silverlake Lounge

Sidewalk: Sidewalk Cafe, East Village

Half Drawn: My friend's apartment on Chula Vista

Hi-Fi: East Village

If You Decide to Leave Your Wife: Spaceland

Two Cigarettes: My apartment on Stanton Street

Love Like That: His apartment in Mid-City

World of Pretend: The Soft Spot, Brooklyn

So Good That We Know: The Bar he didn't walk me home from in the Lower East Side; the room he was renting in West Hollywood

Live This Feeling: His bedroom on Glendale Blvd

You Just Sit There: His apartment on Teviot

Moses: Her apartment on Alta Loma; Chateau Marmont

Pride, The Finale: The Roost, Atwater Village

Weather: My apartment on Valleybrink Road

Buttons: His apartment on Griffith Park Blvd; Three Clubs, Hollywood

Unopened Letter: My apartment in Los Feliz; Ye Rustic Inn; The Party at that house on Hoover

Swim in Defeat: The painting I bought from the bartender on Avenue A; Knitting Factory, NYC

Sahara: Morocco

Playlist

The following songs serve as a soundtrack to this collection. Listen to them on the *Live This Feeling* playlist on Spotify.

Song	Artist
Way I Feel Inside	Lois
So What	Ani Difranco
I'm Only Sleeping	The Beatles
I Figured You Out	Mary Lou Lord
Goodnight, California	Kathleen Edwards
Nightime	Big Star
Samson	Regina Spektor
Connection	Elastica
Pale Blue Eyes	The Velvet Underground
The First Time Ever I Saw Your Face	Roberta Flack
He's Gone	Leona Naess
No Room for Doubt	Lianne La Havas

Song	Artist
Huricane Glass	Catherine Feeny
Portions for Foxes	Rilo Kiley
Maps	Yeah Yeah Yeahs
By Your Side	Beachwood Sparks
Just Like a Woman	Bob Dylan
I Know	Fiona Apple
Like Someone in Love	Bjork
Why Can't I?	Liz Phair
Black	Pearl Jam
Makes Me Wanna Die	Tricky
Break My Heart	Liz Clark
Look At Miss Ohio	Gillian Welch
You're No Good	Linda Ronstadt
Gin	Amy Correia
Nights Like These	Lucero
Sea of Love	Cat Power
I Know It's Over	The Smiths
Silver Springs	Fleetwood Mac

Acknowledgements

Jessica Hoffmann, Ifer Moore, Lauren Kunik, Stacey Van Gorder Leung, Michele Morrow—for your generous availability and assistance with proofreading, editing, brainstorming, and typo-catching throughout the process of putting this collection together.

Megan Neumann, Jillian Cainghug, Jessica Chobot, Kit Scarbo, Sara Feldman, Brooke Olsen, Liz Clark, Joe Rubalcaba, Monique Nijhout, Celine Griscom, Yesenia Montilla, Lee Van Put, and Shauntel Jarreau—for your endless support and encouragement over the years, both in poetry and in life.

Alexandra Franzen and Lindsey Smith—for your guidance during my time in the Tiny Book Course where the idea for this collection came to life.

Nora and Sofia—for your endless love and support.

Everyone who likes & comments on my poetry posts on Instagram and everyone who ever put me up on a poetry stage—THANK YOU!

About The Author

Michelle Bonfils is a poet and lover of strong feelings. Born and raised in Los Angeles, she started performing poetry at open mics in the late 90's. In 2000, she hosted *Spent Sundays* a weekly open mic at Psychobabble Coffee Shop (now Bru Coffeebar) in Los Feliz. While living in New York, she hosted *The Michelle Bonfils Show*, a YouTube program that presented poetry and showcased established and up and coming artists in NYC. When she's not writing poetry, she's spending mornings at coffee shops, talking on the phone with friends, performing at open mics, transcribing her old diaries, and planning her next trip to Paris.

Live This Feeling is her first collection of poetry.

Instagram/Twitter: @MichelleBonfils
Website: www.MichelleBonfils.com

A Note On The Type

This book is set in Adobe Caslon Pro and Viktorie.

www.ingramcontent.com/pod-product-compliance
Lightning Source LLC
Chambersburg PA
CBHW020913080526
44589CB00011B/578